Recovery of Money Paid Under Mistake of Fact
By William A. Keener

© 2018 Phaistos Publishers

THE recovery at law of money paid under mistake affords one of the most striking illustrations of the equitable nature of quasi-contractual obligations, — obligations that are, unfortunately, usually called in our law, contracts implied in law.

Where A intentionally pays money to B, and B intentionally receives it as payment from A, plainly the legal title has passed; and a Court of law, if the money has been paid under a proper case of mistake, compels B to restore to A the money so received, not because the Court does not regard B as the legal owner thereof, but because it is inequitable that he should retain it.

The equitable principle which enables A to recover in this case, as in quasi-contractual obligations generally, is the principle of enrichment: "One shall not be allowed to unjustly enrich himself at the expense of another;" or, as it is usually stated in the common law, "One shall not unjustly profit at the expense of another."

It is proposed in the present article to deal with the general principles under which one is allowed to recover money paid under mistake of fact, and not with their application in detail to specific facts, except so far as it is necessary to a correct understanding of the principles. And the question will be discussed mainly with reference to the remedy at law. Indeed, it has recently been decided[1] by Jessel, M. R., that the sole remedy of a party seeking only to recover money paid under mistake of fact, is at law.

Although an action at law in account to recover money so paid was maintained at an early day,[2] and the right to recover therefor, in indebitatus assumpsit, for money had and received was regarded as settled law in the time of Lord Holt,[3] yet bills in equity have also been maintained.[4] In principle it is impossible to distinguish between fraud and mistake: in each case, if there is no mistake as to identity of parties or subject-matter, a transfer with intent to convey title passes the legal title; and as the legal title is passed with plaintiff's consent without a contract in fact on the part of the person receiving it to transfer it back, the plaintiff's claim, if any he has, must be an equitable one. That fraud and mistake are alike in this respect was recognized by Lord Holt, in Tomkyns v. Barnet.[5] And it is a general principle that equity will not relinquish its jurisdiction, because a Court of law also gives a remedy.[6] In Varet v. N. Y. Ins. Co., supra, Chancellor Walworth says: "The equitable action of assumpsit is now allowed in many cases . . . where the remedy was originally in equity only. But the fact that a remedy exists at law in such cases does not deprive this Court of its ancient jurisdiction to grant relief here." Or, in the language of an English Chancellor, "This Court is not at liberty to give up its jurisdiction because Courts of law have fallen in love with it." It would seem, then, that Jessel's decision cannot be supported, and in this class of cases a Court of equity has concurrent jurisdiction with a Court of law.

What mistake of fact, all other necessary conditions existing, will a Court regard as sufficient?

In Aiken v. Short,[7] Bramwell said: "In order to entitle a person to recover back money paid under a mistake of fact, the mistake must be as to a fact which, if true, would make the person paying liable to pay the money; not where, if true, it would merely make it desirable that he should pay the money."

This remark was not necessary to the decision of the case, and it is submitted that it does not give the proper test. The following illustration would seem to prove that Bramwell's test cannot be adopted. A, supposing that B is indebted to him, though B in fact is not, draws an order on B in favor of C, and delivers it to him as a gift. A dies, and after A's death the order is presented by C, in ignorance thereof, and paid by B, who believes A to be alive; but he knows that he is not indebted to A. B has paid the money supposing that, by so doing, he got a good contract against A. Plainly he has no remedy against A's estate. A's order was a mere offer, which was revoked by A's death,— is C to be a gainer at B's expense? Under Bramwell's test he must be; as the fact about which B was mistaken, namely, A's existence, if true, would not have made B liable to comply with the order.

In Southwick v. First Nat. Bank,[8] a bill drawn by A on B, payable to A's order, was indorsed by A to C, to whom A was indebted, the understanding between A and C being that C should obtain payment of the bill, and extinguish A's indebtedness with the proceeds. The understanding between A and B was that A was to draw a bill on B, and with the proceeds take up an outstanding bill on which A and B were liable. The bill was presented by C to B, who accepted and also paid the bill, under the impression that A was carrying out his part of the agreement. It was held that the mistake of fact was not of a kind to entitle B to recover the money paid. "It is certainly true," says Earl, J., delivering the opinion of the Court, "that if the drawees had known what they now know, or if they had known that the proceeds of the draft were to be applied otherwise than upon the old draft, they would not have accepted or paid the draft. But were they so mistaken that they can retain the money voluntarily paid by them? It is not every mistake that will lay the groundwork for relief. It must be a mistake as to some existing fact, not as to something to happen or to be done in the future. It must be a mistake as to some fact, not remotely, but directly, bearing upon the act against which relief is sought. If it were the rule to relieve against mistakes as to remote, or what are sometimes called extrinsic, facts, great uncertainty and confusion would attend business transactions Here the draft was genuine, addressed to the drawee, who had authorized it to be drawn, and it was held by the defendant, who could lawfully receive payment therefor. There was no mistake as to the intrinsic facts. The facts that the drawers had not acted in good faith with the drawees, or had placed the draft and its proceeds beyond their control, was too remote. The mistake of the drawers was rather as to the application of the money paid by them."

The correct test seems to be suggested in this opinion, namely, the fact about which the mistake is made must not be as to a collateral or extrinsic fact, and the reason for adopting such a test is also suggested in the same opinion, viz., public policy. And public policy requires the adoption of this test, to avoid the uncertainty and confusion that would otherwise attend business transactions. And under this rule of public policy the one person loses and the other gains, not because of the defendant's merits, or the want of merit in the plaintiff, but because to adopt a different rule would endanger business stability. It is because the mistake must not be as to extrinsic or collateral facts that it has been held[9] that if a bank pays, under a mistake as to the state of his account, a check drawn upon it by a depositor, there can be no recovery of the money so paid.

It is difficult to give a test of what is to be considered an intrinsic fact, it being a question which is to be governed by the facts of each case; but a test of this kind would seem to cover most cases. Was the making of the claim against the plaintiff in itself a representation that the party presenting the claim believed in the existence of those facts, about the existence of which the plaintiff was mistaken? If so, the mistake is as to an intrinsic fact.

The mistake must be one about which the plaintiff was not in doubt at the time of payment; for, if he regards the fact as a doubtful one at the time when the claim is made, he cannot be said to have paid under a mistake, but has either paid in settlement of a doubtful claim, or has paid with a view to appearing in litigation as a plaintiff rather than as a defendant, and the law properly says that

it is not for him to choose the time for the beginning of litigation.[10]

On this principle it has been held[11] that a party could not pay a claim which he knew he did not owe, and afterwards recover the money, alleging that he paid because of the loss of his evidence, and that he notified the defendant at the time of payment he should bring an action to recover the money on finding his evidence.

It has been already said that the plaintiff's claim rests on the fact of the defendant being unjustly enriched at the plaintiff's expense.

To make out that the enrichment has been at his expense the plaintiff must show a failure of consideration. It can be properly said that the equity in plaintiff's favor is a failure of consideration rather than mistake, and that in this particular class of cases he establishes his equity, namely, failure of consideration, by showing that he parted with the money without receiving a certain equivalent because of a mistake.

The decision in Taylor v. Hare[12] is an extreme illustration of this position.

In that case the plaintiff sought to recover certain royalties paid to the defendant under a contract by which the defendant agreed to permit the plaintiff to use a certain apparatus, of which they both thought the defendant was the inventor, and for the invention of which the defendant held letters-patent. It was afterwards discovered that the invention was not patentable; but the Court held that the plaintiff could not recover, notwithstanding the fact that the plaintiff laboring under this mistake paid during its user by him a royalty on an apparatus to which he had the same right as defendant, and that the contract was made by him solely in consequence of this mutual mistake. The Court said, although there had been a mutual mistake as to a material point, there was not a failure of consideration. Perhaps the following statement from the opinion delivered by Chambré fairly states the position of the Court: "The plaintiff has had the enjoyment of what he stipulated for, and in this action the Court ought not to interfere unless there be something ex æquo et bono which shows that the defendant ought to refund."

As the plaintiff's claim is founded on a profit at his expense, and as it is a purely equitable claim, the expense must be not simply technically a fact, but also be a fact judged from an equitable standpoint.

In Buel v. Boughton,[13] the plaintiff made a contract, which, in consequence of a mutual mistake, failed to require the payment of interest; and when the obligation matured, he, by mistake, paid principal and interest. It was held that he could not recover back. It is true that the defendant could say in this case that there was no unjust enrichment; but it is also true that the enrichment was not at plaintiff's expense, as it was a contract which could have been reformed in equity, so as to call for the payment of interest. This principle[14] was inequitably applied in Jackson v. McKnight, where the plaintiff, who was indebted to the defendant on an overdue bond, secured by mortgage, paid to the defendant an amount claimed by the defendant as interest. The defendant afterwards assigned the bond and mortgage, and the plaintiff, discovering that no interest was due at the time of said payment, brought an action to recover the money paid under mistake.

It was held that he could not recover. "The difficulty," says Learned, J., delivering the opinion of the Court, "is, that at the time when the plaintiff made this payment he was owing a very much larger amount, overdue and payable, on the very obligation upon which the payment was made. Clearly, if he, the plaintiff, had handed to the defendant $230, to apply on the bond and mortgage, he could not have recovered the sum. But in the present case he claims to recover, because it was intended as a payment of interest, which had in fact been paid, and not as a payment of principal, which had not. The payment, however, was really made on the debt. The plaintiff is, and always will be, entitled to a credit for so much paid thereon. The defendant and the defendant's assignee can enforce the bond and mortgage only for what is payable after crediting this and all other payments. . . . The action to recover money paid by mistake is sustained, because, otherwise, the party would suffer an unjust loss. It should not be extended to cases where the relief is not necessary. It is not necessary in the present case, because the plaintiff can protect himself whenever he is sued on the bond and mortgage."

It is submitted that a different result should have been reached in this case. The money had not been received as part of the principal debt, but as interest, and whatever right the defendant had to apply it in payment pro tanto of the principal debt, if he did not so apply it, but sold the bond and mortgage as a debt entirely unpaid, the simple question is, whether the defendant shall be allowed to retain the money against the plaintiff, against whom he holds it manifestly without consideration, and compel the plaintiff to recover it by using the payment as a counter-claim or set-off against an innocent party, leaving that party to his remedy over against the defendant, or whether the defendant shall be compelled to pay it to the party to whom it will ultimately go, and from whom he received it without consideration. There was no interest to be paid, and the defendant did not apply it to the extinguishment pro tanto of the debt; and the plaintiff's plea in an action brought against him on the bond would be, not payment, but a counter-claim or set-off.

Not only is the expense of plaintiff to be looked at from an equitable point of view, but in deciding whether the enrichment of the defendant is unjust, the question is to be approached in the same way. Hence, if the plaintiff has under mistake paid that which he could not have been compelled to pay either at law or in equity, but which is clearly a moral obligation, there is no unjust enrichment, and the plaintiff is not entitled to relief. "The rule has always been, that if a man has actually paid what the law would not have compelled him to pay, but what in equity and conscience he ought, he cannot recover it back again in an action for money had and received."[15] Hence, if a party should, under mistake of fact as to the date when an obligation matured, pay a claim barred by the Statute of Limitations, he could not recover the money on the ground of mistake.[16] So where A, who purchased a promissory note from the payee before maturity, but by mistake failed to get an indorsement thereof, presented it for payment to the maker, and the maker, supposing that it was duly indorsed, paid it, it was held that he could not recover the money from A, notwithstanding the fact that the payee was largely indebted to him, and was insolvent. The Court said it was not against conscience for A to keep that to which but for a mistake he would have been entitled, both legally and equitably, which, however, owing to a technicality and accident, he could not have collected.[17]

Assuming that the mistake is of a kind recognized by the courts, and that the mistake has resulted in a failure of consideration to the plaintiff, and an enrichment of the defendant, is it an answer to an action brought by the plaintiff, for the defendant to say that the mistake was due to plaintiff's negligence?

In the early cases the judges were undoubtedly ready to hold that a plaintiff who had been negligent could not recover, for there are many dicta to that effect. But by the great current of authority it is held to day that plaintiff's negligence is not sufficient to defeat a recovery.[18] In Lawrence v. American Bank, supra, the Court says: "It is the fact that one by mistake pays money to another to which the latter is not entitled from the former, which gives the right of action, and the fact that the mistake occurs through negligence does not give the payee any better, or the payer any worse, title to the money."

In these jurisdictions where the defendant is allowed to defeat a recovery by showing that he has so changed his position in consequence of the payment that he cannot be put in statu quo, there would seem to be no necessity for invoking the aid of the doctrine of public policy in order to defeat a recovery by a negligent plaintiff. But in a jurisdiction where it is held that it is no defence to an action brought to recover money paid under mistake of fact, that the defendant's position has been changed and substantial rights lost in consequence of the payment, it would seem to be highly inequitable to throw the loss brought about by plaintiff's negligence on the defendant.

Assuming a defendant to be ignorant of plaintiff's mistake, can an action be brought without a demand having first been made upon him? Clearly not on principle. The defendant has a title which the plaintiff gave to him. Can it be said that the defendant has been unjustly enriched at plaintiff's expense, in receiving that which the plaintiff gave to him without any fraud on his part? The unjustifiable enrichment, it is submitted, is not a consequence of the receipt, but of the detention against the will of plaintiff of that which was received with his consent. And the defendant should not be subjected to the costs of an action without having first had an opportunity of restoring that which he lawfully received. It has been so held in England[19] and in New York.[20] In Massachusetts it is held[21] that the cause of action arises immediately upon the payment. If, however, a party receives the money knowing of the mistake, then there is immediately an unjustifiable enrichment, and no demand is necessary.[22]

"When the mistake is mutual, both parties are innocent, and neither is in the wrong. The party honestly receiving the money through a common mistake owes no duty to return it until at least informed of the error. It is just that he should have an opportunity to correct the mistake, innocently committed on both sides, before being subjected to the risks and expenses of a litigation. . . . The necessity of a demand does not, therefore, exist in a case where the party receiving the money, instead of acting innocently, and under an honest mistake, knows the whole truth, and consciously receives what does not belong to him, taking advantage of the mistake or oversight of the other party, and claiming to hold the money thus obtained as his own."[23]

Assuming that, in certain cases, no action can be brought until demand is made, what rules shall be applied in dealing with the Statute of Limitations? The rule ordinarily being that, where a demand is necessary, the Statute of Limitations does not run until demand is made, suppose the plaintiff learns of the mistake soon after the payment of the money to the defendant, is he to be allowed to prolong the defendant's liability indefinitely by failing to make a demand? It would seem not. That which is required of a plaintiff out of regard for the defendant should not be used by the plaintiff to the defendant's disadvantage, when, in denying his right so to use it, nothing inequitable is done. And surely a plaintiff who has it in his power to entitle himself to bring an action at any time cannot complain that he must do so under the penalty of losing his right if it is not exercised within a given period. Stafford v.

Richardson,[24] though not a case of money paid under mistake, was decided on this principle.

Suppose a bill in equity to be filed against an innocent receiver of money paid under mistake. Is it necessary for the plaintiff to make a demand before filing his bill? As a Court of equity, differing from a Court of law where the successful party is entitled, as of right, to costs, can give costs against a successful party, the result of allowing the bill to be filed without a demand is not to impose on the defendant, as is necessarily true at law, a bill of costs in a case where, if his attention had been first called to the matter, an action could have been avoided. Waiving the technical difficulties, which seem to be as great in equity as at law, and the objections of public policy, which would seem to dictate that a Court should not encourage a course which would be productive of unnecessary litigation, the argument of hardship, which is so strong at law, does not prevail in equity. A precedent for allowing the bill to be filed without first making a demand is found in those cases where a contract has been made for the sale of real estate in which there are mutual and concurrent conditions, and where, if either party desires to bring an action at law, he must aver in his declaration and prove on the trial a conditional tender on his part, or a waiver by defendant of such tender. It has been held[25] in such cases that the plaintiff can file his bill in equity for specific performance without first making a demand, with the consequence that, although equity gives him a decree, it awards costs to the defendant. Now, in such a case, it seems as impossible to predicate a breach of contract by the defendant, as it is impossible to predicate of a defendant to whom money has been paid under mistake, an unjust enrichment before a conscious detention thereof. And, unless Courts of equity are willing to recognize the rule in regard to enforcing specific performance without a demand as an anomaly, it would seem difficult to do otherwise than apply the same rules to the case under discussion. The plaintiff's claim being simply an equitable one, the rule that an equity cannot be enforced against a purchaser for value without notice can be invoked by a defendant who has innocently received money paid under a mistake.[26] Although it is beyond the scope of the present article to enter at length upon the question of what constitutes value, it may not be out of place to refer, in this connection, to the case of Newall v. Tomlinson,[27] especially as it is necessary to refer to the case on another point. In that case A and B, each acting for an undisclosed principal, but dealing with each other as principals, entered into a contract whereby A contracted to buy, and B contracted to sell, certain cotton. Weight-lists were furnished by the warehouse-keeper to both A and B. By a mistake made by B's clerk in adding up the figures, the weight appeared to be greater than it really was, and led to an overpayment by A. B at the time of the sale had made advances to his principal on the cotton, and on receiving the money applied it in extinguishment of this indebtedness. After B's principal became insolvent A discovered the mistake, and, B refusing to refund the overpayment, sued for money had and received. It was held that the plaintiff could recover. In behalf of the defendant the rule was invoked that, in the case of money paid under mistake to an agent, there can be no recovery against an agent who has, in ignorance of the mistake, paid the money over to his principal. The Court said that this rule had no application; and on this point the decision is unquestionably sound, for in the case supposed by the counsel, of payment over by an agent, the agent is able to say to the plaintiff, when sued by him, You have no claim against me, as I have done with the money just what you intended I should do, and its receipt by me has not resulted in my enrichment. Whereas, in Newall v. Tomlinson, the money was never paid to plaintiff with the intention that he should pay it over to any one. But as the defendant extinguished, as he was authorized to do, a claim which he held against his principal, he was plainly within the rule of a purchaser for value without notice.[28] If the defendant had gone through the form of giving the money to his principal, and then receiving it back in payment of the debt, clearly he would have been within the rule protecting a purchaser; and yet the difference in form can make no difference in the real nature of the transaction.[29] It seems impossible to support the decision unless on the possible ground that the mistake was made in the first place by the defendant through his clerk; and yet if he was negligent, was not the plaintiff equally so, as he had lists before him which would have enabled him to discover the defendant's mistake? Reference is made by some of the judges to the fact that it was defendant's mistake, but there is no reason for supposing that an absence of that fact would have led to a different decision.

The case also suggests another point: How far is a change of position which prevents the defendant being put in statu quo an answer to an action brought to recover money paid under mistake?

In Newall v. Tomlinson certainly the defendant's position was materially changed in consequence of the payment, and in such a case, if the loss which the defendant will sustain, if the plaintiff is allowed to recover, equals the amount which be has received from the plaintiff, it is difficult to understand how he is unjustly enriched at the plaintiff's expense. If the parties are equally innocent, and the defendant has the title to the money in question, it would seem rather that a Court in taking it away from him unjustly enriches the plaintiff at the defendant's expense.

Of course, if it can be shown that the plaintiff, rather than the defendant, is responsible for the mistake, the defendant, rather than the plaintiff, should bear the loss.

There seems to be little in the way of authority on this point. In Durant v. Ecclesiastical Commissioners,[30] it was held that the defendant's change of position would not prevent a recovery. This is opposed to the dicta found in Freeman v. Jeffries,[31] and is certainly opposed to the dicta contained in many cases in this country.[32]

What constitutes a mistake of fact as distinguished from a mistake of law will be considered hereafter, in discussing the question of the right to recover money paid under a mistake of law.

William A. Keener.

Cambridge.

1. Lamb v. Cranfield, 43 L. J. Ch. 408.

2. Hewer v. Bartholomew, Cro. Eliz. 614.

3. Tomkyns v. Barnet, Skin. 411; Lamine v. Dorrell, 2 L. Ray. 1216.

4. Bingham v. Bingham, 1 Ves. Sr. 126; Neal v. Read, 7 Baxter, 333; First Nat. Bank v. Mastin Bank, 2 McC. 438. See also

Conyers v. Hammond, 2 Cas. in Ch. 81; Pooley v. Ray, 1 P. Wms. 355.

5. Skin. 411.

6. Colt v. Woollaston, 2 P. Wms. 154; Varet v. N. Y. Ins. Co., 7 Paige, 560.

7. 1 H. & N. 210.

8. 84 N.Y. 420.

9. Chambers v. Miller, 13 C.B. N. S. 125. See contra, Merchants' Nat. Bank v. National Eagle Bank, 101 Mass. 281. But compare Boylston Nat. Bank v. Richardson, 101 Mass. 287.

10. McArthur v. Luce, 43 Mich. 435.

11. Windbiel v. Carroll, 16 Hun, 101. Compare, however, Chatfield v. Paxton, 2 East. 471a. Guild v. Balbridge, 2 Swan, 295.

12. 1 B. & P. N. R. 260.

13. 2 Denio, 91.

14. 17 Hun, 2.

15. Ld. Mansfield in Bize v. Dickason, 1 T. R. 285.

16. Bize v. Dickason, 1 T. R. 285 (semble); Hubbard v. City of Hickman, 4 Bush, 204 (semble.)

17. Franklin Bank v. Raymond, 3 Wend. 69.

18. Kelly v. Solari, 9 M. & W. 54; Devine v. Edwards, 87 Ill. 177; Lawrence v. American Nat. Bank, 54 N.Y. 432; Lyle v. Shinnebarger, 17 Mo. Ap. 66 (semble); Guild v. Balbridge, 2

Swan, 295. See, however, West v. Houston, 4 Harr. (Del.) 170; Wilson v. Barker, 50 Me. 447 (semble), contra.

19. Freeman v. Jeffries, L.R. 4 Ex. 189.

20. Southwick v. First Nat. Bank, 84 N.Y. 420.

21. Sturgis v. Perton, 134 Mass. 372.

22. Sharkey v. Mansfield, 90 N. Y. 227.

23. Finch. J., in Sharkey v. Mansfield, supra, at p. 229.

24. 15 Wend. 302.

25. Pomeroy's Specific Performance of Contracts, § 363.

26. See Ins. Co. v. Abbott, 131 Mass. 397; Southwick v. First National Bank, 84 N. Y. 420; Edgerton v. Youmans, 16 Hun, 28.

27. L. R. 6 C. P., p. 405.

28. Ins. Co. v. Abbott, 131 Mass. 397; Southwick v. First National Bank, 84 N. Y. 420.

29. Ins. Co. v. Abbott; Southwick v. First Nat. Bank, supra, at p. 436.

30. 6 Q. B. D. 234.

31 L. R. 4 Ex. 189.

32. Appleton Bank v. McGilvray, 4 Gray, 518; Lawrence v. American National Bank, 54 N. Y. 432; Guild v. Balbridge, 2 Swan, 295.